GALAXY GIRL

ISBN: 979-8-218-42682-8
Imprint: Nebula Books

Cover Design: Anna Love
Interior Illustrations: Anna Love

GALAXY GIRL

by

ANNA LOVE

"I like to tell myself I'm otherworldly.
The truth is, I'm terribly human,
and I'm learning that's a beautiful thing."

—Rachel Finch

I am just a girl

composed of bones

and skin

and stars

the way I tend

to look at things

you'd think

I was

from Mars

I find joy in simple things
like Christmas lights
heartfelt letters
warm blankets
and homemade cookies

I find metaphors in everyday things
like dandelion seeds
drifting towards new life
and butterflies emerging
from their chrysalis
to remind us
that change can be good
even if it seems scary at first

people often say I'm silly
for being so sentimental

but if you don't look at life
with eyes of wonder
how are you supposed
to look at it?

(shoshin)

I wonder
if you're out there

somewhere

wondering
if I'm out there

somewhere

why should my body
define who I am?

the size of my thighs
will not change
the size of my heart
and there is no amount
of makeup on this earth
that will make my mind pretty

(but you don't care about
big hearts and beautiful minds
do you?)

you see my smile
but you don't see my happiness

you hear my voice
but you don't hear my words

you see my tears
but you don't see my pain

you know my present
but you don't know my past

you see my eyes
but you don't see my soul

you read my words
but you don't read my mind

you touch my skin
but you don't touch my heart

you see my scars
but you don't see my wounds

you see my body

but you don't see me

things that are fragile:

flower petals
butterfly wings
feathers
snowflakes
wine glasses
babies
spiderwebs
icicles

and this stubborn
pitter-pattering thing
behind my ribcage

people often wonder why

why I fall in love with music
why I fall in love with words
why I fall in love with strangers
why I fall in love with love

but what else should they expect
from a girl
whose middle name is

Love?

our bones won't be
this strong forever

we cannot live
this long forever

our songs will not
be sung forever

we cannot be
this young forever

growing up
I was always told
not to bring a boy home
if he had piercings
or tattoos
or wild hair
or anything else that
could categorize him
as the stereotypical
punk p.o.s

but I'd rather have a boy
with ink in his skin
and metal in his ears
who treats me like a
queen

over a clean-shaven
suit-and-tie "mr. right"
who treats me like a
pawn

before you say anything
about my thorns

make sure you've seen
my petals

when I was a little girl
I used to run and lock the door
whenever someone I cared about
was preparing to leave
because I thought it would
keep them inside
of course it never worked
and they'd just undo the lock
with a laugh
and be on their merry way
leaving me behind

as I grew older
I stopped locking the door
and let the visitors
come and go
as they pleased
knowing locks were only made
to combat people trying to get in
not out

but when it comes to
my heart
I believe I'll always
keep one hand
over the doorknob

1906

Antoinette sits within the boughs
of an old oak tree
doodling in her diary
as her family searches for her elsewhere
she knows she should be
practicing her piano lessons
but simply cannot make herself
sit in that chair
fluttering her fingers
for hours on end
when she could be
exploring the forest instead
she is the youngest of six sisters
born into a dignified family
and expected to marry as such
and have lots of dignified children
but children can be incredibly fussy
and the men are often no better
a lot is expected of her these days
but she can hardly keep up
with everyone's expectations
without feeling winded
which is why she prefers to hide
among the trees
humming songs into the wind
and daydreaming of being
someone worth remembering
someday

even if it isn't in a way
anyone anticipates

"do you really think that
out of seven billion people
on this planet
none of them will be
compatible with you?"

"do you really think that
out of seven billion people
on this planet
I will be enough
to satisfy one person?"

I was never a normal teenager
I've never had a sleepover
or even a best friend
I've never had a boyfriend to hold my hand
or go on milkshake dates with
I've never had the chance
to hang out at the mall
or flash peace signs
in front of graffitied walls
or take aesthetic polaroids
in a back alley at 2 a.m.
or go to a Saturday night house party
only to leave after a half hour
because everyone was drinking
and things were getting messy
I've never had someone
to tell my secrets to or dance with
under the light of a disco ball
or go to the movies with
while we smuggle candy
in our jacket sleeves
I've never been in the backseat
while a group of girls
drove down dirt roads
blasting modern country
and shouting at the stars
or tagged along on spontaneous trips
to the beach just because we were bored

and maybe this is not even
what normal teenagers do
but one of the hardest things
I've ever had to face
is the fact that I will never
be able to find out

(anemoia)

my heart
is too big

and my soul
is too old

for my body

(defect)

we all have wings

but we're too scared to fly

afraid we'll crash

so we don't even try

tell me

would they still
look at you the same
if the camera
was turned off
and the filter
fell away
from your face?

when I was mere stardust
floating in the milky way
I knew I wanted to be
love and light
in human form someday

and the story goes
that when I was a small being
cradled inside my mother's womb
I held up two tiny fingers
for three women watching me
on the ultrasound screen

I was barely a woman myself
yet I still gave them the sign
that I was destined
to be a peacemaker
once I was born into
this troubled world

(perhaps I was a hippy
even in the cosmos)

I am not like other girls

that is

my advantage

but mostly

my downfall

if Mary Jane had a face
what would she look like?

if she had a voice
what would she sound like?

if she had a checklist
what would her goals be?

and if she asked
to stay with you for a while

would you let her in?

I love writing

I love how I can
make images flash
in people's minds
with only a few words
how I can make pain
sound pretty
how I can make
a work of art
simply from thought
how I can look around me
and find inspiration
at every corner
how I can immortalize
the ones who have
given me these words
hiding them within
metaphors
and turning them
into history

how I can speak
with a pen
much better than
with my tongue

sometimes I am taken aback
by the simple yet profound
beauty of this world
and everything inhabiting it

like sunshine filtering through trees
clouds forming shapes in the sky
flowers blooming through concrete cracks
the wind playing with your hair
stars twinkling in the sky
seashells submerged in sand
rainbows piercing storm clouds
snowflakes sticking to your lashes
soft peaches in summer
good music making you dance
laughing from your belly
two people falling in love
kittens rubbing against your ankles
the smell of lavender

and the warm faith in your soul
that everything will happen
the way it was destined to

(philocaly)

it saddens me
to know that
in today's society

speaking from your heart
won't get you nearly
as much attention

as taking a picture
in front of
a bathroom mirror

so much
is often said

but so little
is ever done

(procrastination)

if I can't convince anyone
to be my friend
then how am I ever
going to convince anyone
to fall in love with me?

(shower thoughts)

some days
I am the sun

some days
I am the storm

on the hardest days
I am both

painting the sky
with rainbows

music
on its own
is poetry

it makes us dance
it makes us sing
it makes us cry
it makes us hope
it makes us angry
it makes us laugh
it makes us remember
it makes us love

and
like all good poetry
it makes us feel
alive

I wonder
what goes through
your mind

as you wonder
what goes through
my mind

some people believe
that they are
walking through life
with eyes wide open

but oh
how blind they are

I wish I could find
my soul mate
while I'm young
so I could grow with him
learn with him
love him
and snatch him up
before he gives himself away
to too many girls
that are not me

sometimes
it's hard to tell
the difference
between

inspiration

and

intimidation

my father
is multicolored

which is to say
that he has two
different-colored eyes

which is to also say
that he has two
different-colored personalities

(though I was
never enough
for either of them)

just because I don't
pry open my mouth
dust the cobwebs
from between my teeth
and just talk
like a normal person
doesn't mean I never
speak

don't you ever wonder
why there is always
a pen in my hand?

I don't care how gorgeous
you believe yourself to be

if you have an ugly heart

you are hideous

1983

Angela is sitting on the couch
with a science book in her lap
while the radio plays "Africa"
watching as a boy with pizza stains
on his woolly striped sweater
and a superfluous amount
of hairspray slicking back
his otherwise curly dark hair
dances in front of the television
missing every beat
but still confident in his moves
her mother is in the kitchen
baking a green bean casserole
her father is in the basement
playing pool with his friends
from the country club
her little sister plays with
Barbies and plastic ponies
in the room down the hall
and Angela sways back and forth
to the music
hoping that life for her
will always be
this simple and sweet

sure

there may be
plenty of fish
in the sea

but I walk on
land

do not be disheartened
if someone calls you
a crybaby
it does not mean
you are childish
it simply means
that your soul is gentle
and that you have a heart
made of sugar
instead of stone
vulnerable
sensitive
these are not bad things
they are good things to be
in a world full of people
who won't open
their own hearts
(or tear ducts)
it means you hurt
you care
you feel injustice
clenching your heart
like a flaming fist
and sometimes
if you are brave enough
you can turn your tears
into triumph

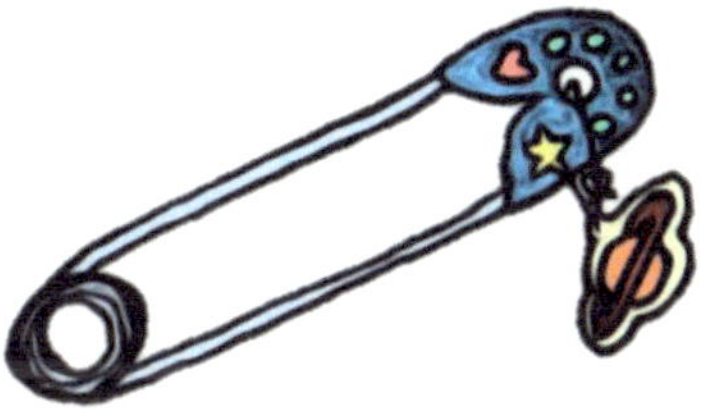

everyone around me
is living life
in the fast lane

and as I watch them
pass by in a blur

all I'm doing
is standing still
at the crosswalk

even in a crowded room
she felt so lonely

no

especially
in a crowded room

do
not
let
your
favorite
songs
be
ruined
because
of

them

some days
we find ourselves stuck
in a perpetual loop of

once I finish this
I will feel better

and

I cannot finish this
because I feel bad

these days
we must be strong
and remember
that even mountains
can be moved
with a gentle nudge

it can be
warm and understanding

or

cold and heartbreaking

(silence)

1985

Angela is looking for canned soup
as "Take On Me"
plays in the mini-mart
her mother pushes a cart in front of her
gold hoop earrings
jangling in tandem with her fast strides
as she rushes down the aisle
her sister dances terribly behind her
her frizzy red hair flying
and her plaid skirt swishing
their father tells them to behave
but they don't
they snap their gum
and click their boots in rebellion
beginning to sing the chorus
as loud as they can
unable to contain their giggles
between words and cans of Campbell's

the world stares at them
and their matching plaid skirts
in disapproval
but they do not care

they just dance

this silent life

is getting

so loud

in my ears

(tinnitus)

according to the internet
a poet is described as:

a person possessing
special powers
of imagination
or expression

well done Google

darling
I'm not trying to be
better than *you*

I'm trying to be
better than *your*
expectations of *me*

I look at a cute couple
holding hands
by the Ferris wheel
and wonder if their
relationship
is as strong
as their wristbands

I look at the girls
who sashay past me
half-dressed
in lace and leather
and wonder if by
exposing themselves
they are just trying to
cover up their insecurities

I look around
the fairgrounds
realizing how
most of the rides
are made for two people
and wonder if the loners
will ever feel less lonely
even as they smile
on the other side
of the fence

I catch a glimpse
of myself
in a distorted mirror

and wonder
if anything
is ever as it seems

something within me is
desperately
searching
reaching
clawing
for something
it is unable to name
but cannot stop
striving towards

and I don’t think
it will ever
be able to stop

(sehnsucht)

I have a hard time
letting go of things

that's why I still
wear my favorite socks
long after I have worn
holes in the toes

that's why I still keep
text messages
from my favorite people
years after they have
been sent

that's why I document
every aspect of my life
as if it were all just
one big journal

because if I do not
keep any of it
it will be as if
it never happened

hey Alexa
can you give me a hug
and tell me that everything
is going to be okay?

(I didn't think so)

poets

need

pain

like

roses

need

rain

(growth)

when he was younger
he used to think that
poets were silly
to feel so strongly
about simple things
like cinnamon
forests
rainbows
sunsets
cherry blossoms
snowflakes
clouds
the blind faith that love
is always waiting for us
just around the corner

only after falling in love
with these things himself
did he realize that he had been
the silly one all along

does the beat

of a heart

keep the music alive

or

does the beat

of the music

keep a heart alive?

(rhythm)

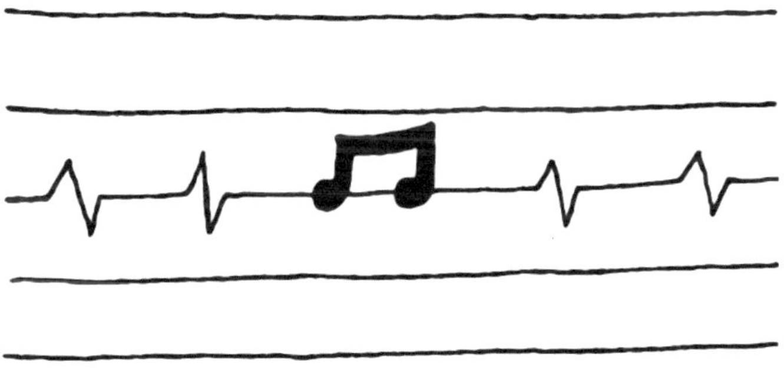

it is quite concerning

just how much

a wireless internet connection

is more feverishly

sought after

than human connection

(what's the password?)

I do not pine for people
to tell me I have
a beautiful face
it is something I've heard
many times
and it means next to nothing

I long for the individuals
who take a look at me
and are able to see past
my sparkling eyes
to the vulnerable soul
that only comes out
when she is comfortable
to the inner child
that likes playing with bugs
and other unloved things
to the girl
made of scars and stars
looking for a place to belong

to say I have
a beautiful mind
is the greatest compliment
I could ever receive

I don't just write poetry
nor do I just read poetry
I feel it
I taste it
I revel in it
because poetry
is more than mere words
poetry is life
condensed into sentences
feelings disguised as metaphors
it is heartbreak
and joy
and nostalgia
all in a single paragraph
it is a song
a voice
a soft whisper
spilling secrets
and sending subliminal messages
that only I can understand

the poets are trying to tell us something
every single one of them

and I am determined
to listen
to learn
to be

(scripturient)

everywhere I go
I hear

"talk to your doctor about (insert medication)"
and
"ask your doctor if (insert medication) is right for you."

what this world needs
is more hugs and less drugs
more caring and less comparing
more understanding and less reprimanding
more

"ask your doctor if peace of mind is right for you,"
and
"talk to your doctor about love."

prescription options:
writing in a self-care journal
cuddling a cat
reading a book
painting or drawing
taking a walk in nature
playing a cozy video game
listening to your favorite music
spending time with loved ones

side effects may include:
motivation
happiness
creativity
gratefulness
peace
faith
love
confidence

"never change for the world,

never let the world change you,

and most important of all,

never stop smiling."

(words from a dear friend)

1986

Angela looks through a row
of sequins and silk
while "Girls Just Wanna Have Fun"
plays in JC Penney
homecoming is in a few days
and a group of girls
with glittery scrunchies in their hair
laugh at her from across the aisle
the dresses they'd picked out
draped over their arms
she tries to ignore them
but each snap of their gum
is like a gunshot
and she is all too aware
of her worn out shoes
and the fraying edges
of her mother's old blouse
she takes a sip
of her cherry Slurpee
to cool the heat
rising in her cheeks
and rushes to the nearest fitting room
where no one but her own reflection
can witness her break down

because she is a nobody now

because she doesn't even
have a date for the dance

because she lost everything

they try to compliment me
by telling me that I am
a “rare breed”

but they don’t understand
just how lonely
rare can be

I used to believe that
poetry had to rhyme
that it required precise stanzas
and organized hyperboles
and lots of elegant words
that no one ever knows
the definition of
in order to properly be called
poetry

now I realize that poetry can be
messy words spat onto paper
in outbursts of emotion
in the middle of the night
a single sentence
a single thought
a single feeling
sometimes just a single word
that grabs hold of your heart
and refuses to let go
until it is felt
until it is heard
until it is understood

until it is released

(catharsis)

when will I not

get butterflies

from someone who

gets butterflies

from someone else?

I have always been wary of the darkness
shying away from pitch-black rooms
and vacant streets
where bats and ominous voices
come out of the shadows
to get tangled up in my hair
as I try to make my way home

but as of late
I'd almost welcome a shadow creature
to pay my bedroom a visit
in the witching hour
to creep out from under my bed
grab me by the bare ankles
and drag me down
into a dark and exciting new world
far far away
from this mediocre light

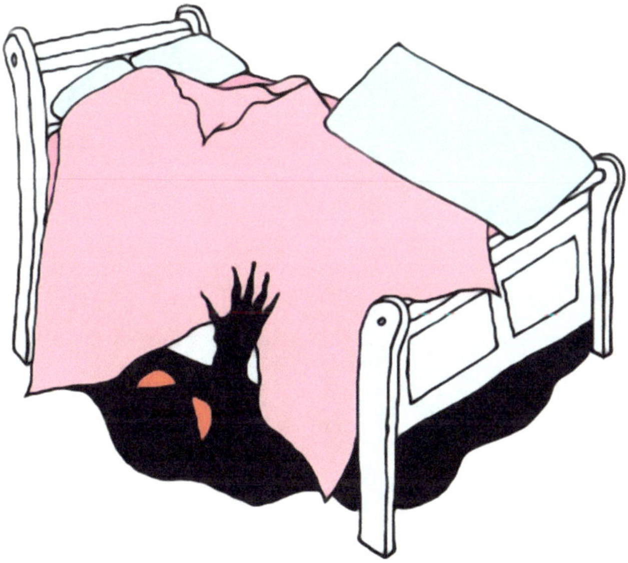

I like to tell myself
that I have galaxies in my eyes
planets on my skin
and stardust in my veins
only to mask the bitter truth
that I am a mere
dimly-lit star

unnoticeable

lost
in a constellation
of billions

2009

Anna is riding shotgun
in her aunt's rusting Jeep
and munching on the crab rangoon
she'd snuck out of
the Chinese restaurant
in her jacket pocket
"More Than A Feeling"
her first favorite song
comes on the rock station
and she bounces in her seat
as her aunt turns up the volume

they sing along
as they cruise through town
careless and free
and full of sesame chicken

and life is good

we kill time

and in return

time slowly kills us

birds in cages
are often thought to be happy
because they spend their days
singing and dancing away

but we cannot understand
their melancholic language
the panic laced into their trills
the sadness seeping through their tweets

and their crestfallen cries for help
disguised as music

for the freedom
just beyond the bars

one day
I would like my words
to be great
to be known
to be loved
to be alive
to be read by someone
who needed to hear them
or maybe even tattooed
on paper skin
displayed forever by someone
who understood
what I was trying to say

but until then
they will be kept safe
in my notebook
alive nonetheless

maybe my soul remembered you
from a lifetime ago when love was true
we'd drink coffee and tea and sit on the terrace
of a glamorous building in the heart of sweet Paris

perhaps we were foxes playing tag in a field
a prince and a pauper with feelings concealed
we could have been stars shining bright in the sky
or wildflowers picked by passerby

we could have been thunder rumbling loud in clouds
while now we're just faces unfamiliar in crowds
what we once were we cannot be again
or maybe we can just who knows when

perhaps when we're fish in the deep blue sea
I'll tell you the story about you and me
how once in our lives we had made works of art
how once in our lives we had been kept apart

I'll have you again in the Eiffel tower
or growing beside me as a neighbor flower
but for now I'm a poet and you have no clue

that my soul will always remember you

(wonderwall)

my mind is such a maelstrom
of stars and scars
that no astronomer in their right mind
should ever dare to explore it

still
I hope there is at least one
crazy space-lover out there somewhere
willing to take the plunge

my mother took a trip to New York
for the fourth of July
and for a week
my social media
was flooded with photos
of her adventures
in the marvelous metropolis

only the finest mixed drinks
sipped under skies
full of fireworks
only the finest parties on balconies
where laughter and music
drowned out everyday sorrows
only the finest hotel suites
where she could lounge
like a model in a magazine

and all I got
when she returned
was a keychain

to be a poet
is to render yourself vulnerable
and expose your soul

to let your heart
do the talking
instead of your brain

to let out
what you have been holding in
for so long

to trust that someone
somewhere
will understand

to be a poet
is to be
brave

the girl in the mirror
is constantly changing
shifting
growing

every day
I meet myself
with a brand new face

and that terrifies me
and excites me
all at once

just because you don't
advertise your body
in front of a bathroom mirror

just because you don't have
dozens of thirsty men
in your direct messages

just because you don't
take aesthetic photos
of everywhere you go
and everything you eat
and everything you buy
and everything you do

doesn't mean your life
or yourself
is any less valid
but perhaps more so
because you are
living for yourself
and not for the validation
of strangers on a free app
that means next-to-nothing
at the end of the day

knowing that the soul meant for mine
is wandering this earth at this very moment
looking for me in the face
of every girl he meets

is one of the happiest

and saddest

things I could ever imagine

pardon me if I may seem
as cynical as I sound

I'm just sad that fat-bottomed personalities
don't make the world go 'round

there is a method
to my madness

a salvation
in my sadness

I would much rather have
all of the kind words
all of the company
all of the flowers
all of the memories
and all of the appreciation
for my life

while I am still alive

rather then
when I am not

they say you can't take back
the things you do in life

but fail to mention
that you also can't take back
the things you *don't* do

when I was a little girl
my mother told me that
I would never be able to
get a boy to want me
unless I wore makeup
that if I were to be put beside
a dolled-up drama queen
the boy would not pick me
because I wasn't pretty enough
without the help of cosmetics
he would pick the Barbie girl
not caring about my dull
colorless face or the treasures
hiding just under the surface
because
I
just
wasn't
pretty
enough

(over a decade later
I'm left wondering
if her words
weren't true after all)

one day
everything feels like
starlight and dewdrops
and you are standing
on top of the world

then the next day
you are standing
in the middle of a storm
knowing it will go away
if you just
think about something else

(anxiety)

will there ever
be a time
in my life

when someone
can look at me

and not
want to
change something?

if we
don’t leave
this town

then we
will surely
drown

sometimes I wonder
where is he

the soul out there
who is meant for me?

I’m destined to meet him
to be his wife

and for him I will search
for the rest of my life

my blessing:

I can turn anything
into poetry

my curse:

I turn everything
into poetry

2015

Anna sits in a doctor's office
on a cloudy afternoon
her world crumbling to pieces
to the tune of "Jar Of Hearts"
she tucks her shaking hands
under her thighs
as a tear slides down her cheek
and the room slightly sways
or maybe that's just her
rocking herself back and forth
a natural instinct to calm oneself
she closes her eyes against
the bright white lights
interrogating her
and she wonders
what she has ever done
in this life or the ones before
to deserve such punishment
such a life-sentence
of incurable pain and suffering

what has she ever done
that was so unforgivable
that judgement had to
follow her through time

and hit her
when she least
expected it?

I promise
I can show you
the sweetest form of Heaven

if you promise
to bear with me
through the most bitter Hell

I have yet to be convinced
that I am not actually a star spirit
reincarnated as a human girl

for I am so much different
than everyone else

it's as if my being shines so bright
it hurts their eyes
and I speak a foreign language
they are unable to understand

(monachopsis)

dear woodland wanderer:

do you even realize
how special you are?
there you go
humming songs
while foraging for humanity
in a world
destined to destroy itself
digging up dead flowers
and planting healthy ones
in their place
hugging trees
and helping bees
and worshiping mother nature
as the great goddess she is
forging new paths
through thickets as thorny
as midnight thoughts
and making the world
a better place
simply by being
yourself

(werifesteria)

we keep telling ourselves

"maybe someday this will happen"
"maybe someday I'll do this"
"maybe someday I'll see that place"
"maybe someday things will get better"

maybe someday
we'll be able to stop saying

"maybe someday"

there is a restlessness in my soul
that nobody seems to understand

it is a deep yearning
an incessant ache in my bones
for something I cannot name

a feeling so fierce
it bruises my skin
trying to escape my body

it is a tingle on my tongue
always threatening
to break through my teeth

it is a beast that has been
kept dormant for quite some time
just waiting for the right moment
the wonderful opportunity to rise
and shake the earth with its power

the bad thing about
distancing yourself from everyone

is when you look over your shoulder
and realize

they haven't even noticed
how far away you've wandered

"I hope we last forever,"
my mother sighed on a carnival ride
a wide grin on her face
as she gazed with adoration
at the latest catch
she'd reeled in
with her siren song

turns out
forever is subjective
and some fish
are better left in the sea

I am grateful I didn't have
the internet and social media
when I was growing up
to fry my fragile little mind
with insecurities
violence
profanity
vulgarity
and political propaganda
I had coloring books
Barbie dolls
daytime cartoons
something called the outdoors
and the ability to learn things
at my own pace
at the appropriate age
without being prematurely exposed
to things my innocent brain
could not correctly grasp
as a budding little blossom

(late bloomer)

how ironic it is

that being vulnerable

is perhaps the purest form

of strength

2016

Anna stumbles over her own feet
as she walks towards her first crush
whom she's never spoken a word to
and who has no idea she exists
"Sleeping With A Friend"
plays in the grocery store
as she forces herself to speak
asking him where she can find
instant banana pudding
although she knows this store
like the back of her hand

she follows him a few aisles down
and politely thanks him
for his "help"
he smiles and skips away
his feet hitting the ground
in tandem with her racing heart
and though he didn't say much
he said something
which is more than nothing

and as he disappears
around the corner
she clutches the Jell-O box
to her chest
and dances away
into the unknown

we come into this world
kicking and screaming

and that is how
we shall leave it

ever since the crow
heard the wistful croon
of the owl
as she sang a lullaby
to the fox
one starry night

she has hated
the sound
of her own hoarse voice

you know that feeling you get
when you hear your favorite song?
the goosebumps
the adrenaline
the serotonin
the sudden burst of stars
exploding in your chest?
the irresistible urge
to turn up the volume
and sing as loud as you can
or dance until you drop
because it makes you happy
in ways words could never explain?

think about what you want
to do with your life
where you want to be
who you want to be
and whatever gives you that
"favorite song" feeling

unearth your passion
no matter how deep
you have to dig
and once you find it
make sure you chase after it

run so fast no one can catch you
and dedicate every breath you take
to what makes you happy

a mother
a sultry siren

a father
a manic sailor

a daughter
just trying to find
her proper place
among the waves

I was driving down the highway
admiring a strawberry sunset
and thinking to myself

what if I don't find my soul mate?
what if I do?
will he want to travel?
will he want to make art?
will he see life through eyes like mine?
will he want to learn as much as he can
in our short time on this planet?
will he live instead of just breathe?
is he out there somewhere
wondering the same thing about me?
is he even out there at all?
will he ever find me
or will he be too busy
living his own glorious life?

then I realized
perhaps my lust for life
was beginning to overpower
my lust for love

you cannot have
an outer revolution

without
an inner evolution

I know I'm
just a girl

but can I
change the world?

sometimes
we don't get what we want

and sometimes
we don't want what we get

but sometimes
that's okay

no matter what the crow
may say
or think
or do

she will always hope
that the fox
and the owl
will stay together
and be happy
be free
be soft and light
and lost in laughter

even if she has to
stay behind
submerged in shadows

even if there are
diamonds
glistening in her eyes

(even if she has to
use metaphors)

the stars must look down on us
from their crystalline thrones
in the sky
and think

"what strange creatures they are"

I will apologize
for many things

but poetry
will never be
one of them

*(sorry
not sorry)*

2019

Anna is alone in a big house
as snow falls outside
fuzzy socks pulled over her feet
to keep her warm
she dances in the middle
of the living room floor
pretending that a brown-eyed boy
is dancing with her
"I Don't Dance"
plays in her ears
as she spins around in circles
her fingers wrapped around
the hand of a ghost
a ghost that whispers nice things
but never shows his face
a ghost that tastes sweet
but leaves a bitter aftertaste

a ghost
that doesn't even dance

I say I’ve got galaxies stuck in my hair
that I’m borne from the stars
that I don’t have a care

but deep down inside
I’m a very small girl
who is just trying to find her place in this world

it has been said
that one of the hardest things
we will ever have to do
is mourn a person
who is still alive

and I will admit
I sometimes wear black
for people who still
walk the earth

my love ranges from
sentences to novels

there is no
in-between

sometimes I'm not sure
if I am the only one awake
in a sleeping world

or if I am the only one dreaming
in a world with eyes wide open

"just don't think about it."

I don't think you understand
poets cannot afford to simply
"not think about it"
because it is our duty
to think
to feel
to pick our scabbing emotions to pieces
until we have gathered
every ounce of feeling we can
from the injuries

otherwise
poetry would not exist
would it?

they tell me that I am
a rare and precious jewel
and that rare and precious jewels
are hard to find

but that's the thing

they are difficult to discover
even if they are residing
right under your nose
which is oftentimes the case
for people who tend to look
in all the wrong places

(will I ever be found?)

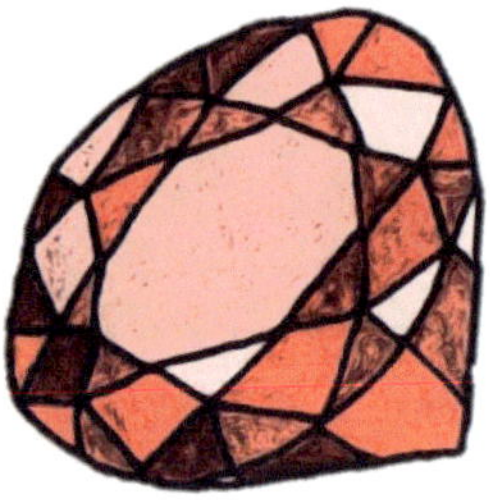

I cannot stop myself
from growing older

but I am trying my best
to prevent myself
from growing colder

(the warmth within)

some walls

only have

ears

when they

want to

instead of saying
"those were the days,"

start by saying
"these are the days."

(narrative)

I am so many things

condensed and molded
into the shape
of a small human

and sometimes
I just don't know
what to do with myself

you

are

what

you

~~eat~~
~~think~~
~~write~~
~~read~~
~~speak~~
~~believe~~
~~wear~~
~~say~~
~~do~~

are

I fell in love
with darkness

I fell in love
with light

both hindered
my vision

and made me
lose my sight

before you say anything
about my petals

make sure you've seen
my thorns

mama always said
not to trust good looks
and go for a man with money

she said love's not like
it is in the books
it's not all roses and honey

we all live on a giant planet
floating in the middle of nowhere
orbited by a big ball of gas
and a rock that reflects its light
71% of that planet
is covered in the deepest waters
and only 95% of those waters
have been explored by us
we all live on a giant planet
where ancient monuments stand
with no one knowing
how they came to be
and the plant life can either
heal us or harm us
where animals and humans alike
decide to travel in their own packs
shunning outsiders even though
we all breathe the same air

we all live on a giant planet
where nearly 30,000 trees
are cut down each day
where 78% of marine life
is at risk of choking on plastic
where humans collectively toss out
25 trillion Styrofoam cups in a single year
where 100 million tons of garbage
is just floating in the ocean

this planet was never ours
but we're definitely making sure
that one day
it won't be able to be
anything else's either

if only
cupid knew

what pain
he's caused

with his
little arrows

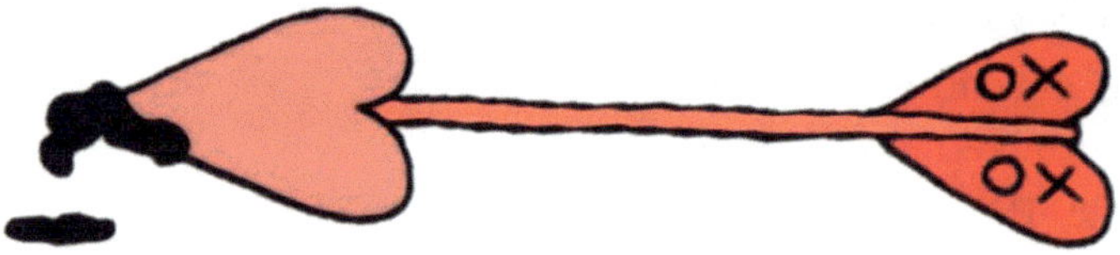

when we're constantly juggling

the good and the bad

sometimes we forget

which we hold in our hands

a true friend is not someone
you merely take pictures with
and brag about on social media
not just another name in your "friends" list
not someone you see every day
or even talk to every day
not someone you match outfits with
and feed gossip to

a true friend is someone who will
always be there for you no matter what
someone who will pick up the phone
and manage to turn your tears into laughter
someone whose voice you can listen to
for nearly three hours straight
even though you hate talking on the phone
someone who comes to your graduation
even though he has to walk all the way there
someone who recognizes a fellow old soul
when he stumbles across one
someone who speaks words of wisdom
as if he were talking to his offspring
someone who deserves so much more
than what life has given him

a true friend doesn't try to change you
but instead encourages you
to always remain your authentic self
to never let the world rain on
your sunshine smile
to never turn sour just because
someone thought you were too sweet

and a true friend
will spend her entire morning
stringing these words together
just so he might understand
his impact on her life

she sits in the corner
with a notebook in her lap
blending into the background
and quietly giggling to herself
as people walk around her
not knowing that they
are in the presence
of galaxies
wrapped up in human skin

(not knowing that they
are galaxies themselves)

if you ever feel bad about yourself
because you believe you are not
as beautiful as the rose
that gets all the attention

remind yourself that you are
as beautiful as the mighty lotus
that blooms upon the surface
of all the murky waters
that try to stunt its growth

(oubaitori)

to make a poet angry
is to tickle the nose
of a sleeping dragon
to throw a burning torch
into the center of a serene forest
to stand at the base
of a dormant volcano
and dare it to erupt over
everything that lies below

to make a poet angry
is to ignite a fire
that will burn forever
on yellowed pages
singeing hearts
for generations to come

(hope you brought
some marshmallows)

"why do you think so fondly of me?"

"because you're you."

2019

Anna is wedged between her grandparents
in an old rickety truck
bumping down a washboard road
because they wanted to see the sunset
from a better angle
the sky is bright and colorful
in the approaching twilight
her favorite time of day
and fields of tall grass swaying in the breeze
become peppered with flickering fireflies
no music is needed because
for once
the peaceful sound of
crickets and crunching gravel is enough
adding to the serene beauty
of the countryside

she leans her head back
and smiles into the night
at the glimmering stars above
and her heart that is filled with love

and in this moment
life is good again

in this generation
real compliments are rare
I would rather hear a guy tell me
that I have a beautiful soul
and not just a beautiful face
that I am inspiring
and not just appealing
that I am soul food
and not just eye candy
that he likes my heart
and not just the skin concealing it
that I am everything
he could never understand
but that's okay
because we have the rest of our lives

until then
I will mind my busy little business
and write my silly little stories

as the guys who chase after girls
just because they are "thicc baddies"
run right past me

if you ever feel like
there is too much stardust
in your bones
please do not cut yourself open
and empty it out for people
who are incapable of
understanding you
in your entirety
instead
let it seep from your skin
in gentle waves
and maybe these parts of you
will be what fills another's
empty bones

maybe these parts of you
will be what saves their life

(sharing is caring)

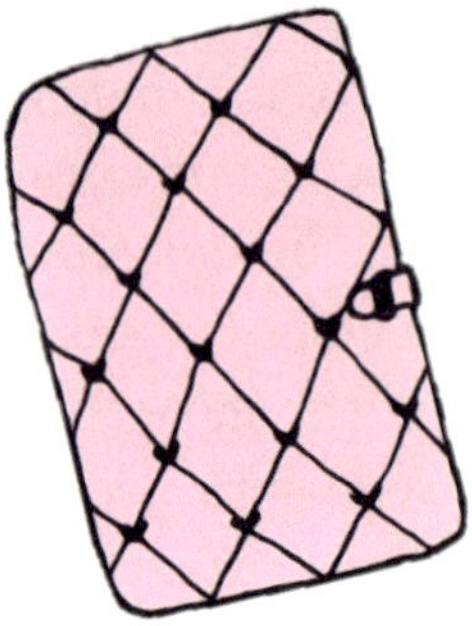

when I was a young girl
I kept a journal in my room
and would write in it daily
of the good
the bad
and the mundane
often creating run-on sentences
made up of misspelled words

when I was a young adolescent
I left behind that big pink book
yet would often find myself
jotting down my hormonal thoughts
within the confines of cheap textbooks
and though my grammar
was much neater
my headspace was not

even now
as a young adult
I spill my heart and soul
onto whatever suitable writing tool
happens to be the most convenient
at the time a perfect poem strikes
but even perfect poems
still tend to be messy now and then

and it took me
all these years
all these books
all these poems
to realize
I've been a writer all along

I once heard the phrase:

"stop searching
for your other half
because you are not
a half."

and it's true
you are whole on your own
a masterpiece in motion
and though a special someone
might fill an empty space
you are not incomplete
just because you are single
just because you have not
found a forever lover
doesn't mean you are
any less worthy of living
you are not walking around
with a hole in your heart
unless you believe it to be so
in which case you should
fill yourself with things
that bring you the utmost joy
and maybe one day
when you least expect it
you will step into a fairytale
in which you stumble upon
the sweetest prince (or princess) charming
and will live happily ever after together

Rapunzel did it
Cinderella did it
even Ariel did it

but if you have not yet
there's nothing wrong with that

I don't know when
or even how it happened
but one day I looked in the mirror

really looked close at this girl
whom I hadn't liked very much before

and as a smile spread across
both of our faces
I thought

she doesn't seem so bad after all
I'd love to get to know her

sometimes life decides to
bring us out of
our comfort zone

and sometimes
we realize that
things make so much more sense
from the outside

life tip:

focus on your future

more than your past

sometimes Sadness comes to me
a lonely entity aching to be understood
an empty apparition yearning to be whole
everyone else pushes her away
but instead I embrace her like a friend
and let her stay with me
until she has decided it is time
for her to move on

and though my days are
much better during her absence
I will always wait with open arms
for the day she returns to me

(because she will)

they will tell you

they want to give you

the world

but only if it

r e v o l v e s

around them

I will always be a poet

even when I cut myself open
and nothing comes out

even when these thoughts
cannot set themselves straight

even when this ink
refuses to form words

even when these empty pages
are determined to remain blank

I will always be a poet

I've had people apologize to me
for talking too much
say they are sorry for
"wasting my time"
and every time
I grab them by the collar
and urge them to continue
telling their stories because
I know all too well
what it's like to not talk
fearing my words
will not find a home
at their destination
I will not turn a blind ear
on someone who likes to talk
even if I do not say a word
even if I cannot keep up with
so many spinning tales
even if all I do is sit
quietly listening
as they ramble on and on

I will be what they need:
someone to talk to
to listen
to remember
to understand

I looked into the mirror
at the doctor's office today
and couldn't believe
what I saw before me

I turned in a circle
and smiled
because
for once
I didn't hate my body

(it's a shame I had to
shed thirty pounds
before I considered myself
beautiful)

“there is nothing
you can ever do in life
to make me any more
proud of you
than I already am,

for what we do
is nothing
compared to who we are.”

(graduation)

I’ve often been told
that I have beautiful eyes
that they sparkle in the sun
and hold the light
of divinity

but I’ve never been more proud
as I was when I was told
that they sparkle the most
when I am angry
that they blaze with shooting stars
when blood boils under my skin
and strike down anyone who
happens to be caught
in their crosshairs
with just a single look

(if looks could kill)

life isn't just another
video game to be won
we can't choose our characters
we can't set the difficulty level
we don't get a tutorial
or even a pause menu
it's not easy to level up
we can't simply save our progress
to ensure everything stays intact
we cannot collect extra lives
along the way
nor can we use cheat codes
to make things easier
we can't just run to another save file
when things get rough
we can't just erase
the mistakes we make
and we can't just overwrite our past
with the push of a button
there is no leaderboard here
not really
because at the end of the day
we all end up in the same place
it doesn't matter who gets there
first or last
because the finish line
may not be as glorious as you might think

life is not a video game
where you are constantly in control

but this is not a poem telling you
that you are powerless
when it comes to your life either

(PRESS START)

I may not be able

to turn your head

as quick as the other girls

but I will definitely

turn you

into poetry

if you let me

"I can see you as being someone
who will be remembered,"
my grandfather says one evening
while I'm making macaroni
"you just have to be
more confident in yourself."

"I kind of want to be
someone like that," I mumble
my eyes downcast
"or try to be anyway."

"do you *kind of*
want to *try to be*
someone like that
or do you *want to be*
someone like that?"
he asks
slightly slurring his words
which smell like
secrets and spiced rum

I stand up straight
as I stir the pot
"I *do.*"

"then do it!" he says sternly
his eyes boring into mine
"and don't ever let anyone
try to change you
or the direction you're heading in."

some days I am not
all sunflowers and lemonade
preaching peace into the world
some days I am a mere caterpillar
wrapped up in a chrysalis
of warm blankets
and trying to stop
the ocean in my eyes
from kissing the shores
of my cheeks
I am not always
as light and sugary
as I portray myself to be
for behind my galactic curtain
lies a great heaviness
that sometimes feels impossible
to bear

~~diseases~~
~~disorders~~
~~disappointments~~

some days
I am like the moon
either whole
a fraction of myself
or eclipsed altogether

but underneath the darkness
I still shine

poetry

will always be

my favorite

coping mechanism

sometimes
the thing we have been craving
for so long
suddenly shows up at our door
as if it was always a part of us
and is simply returning home
after a long journey

and sometimes
we don't even realize it is home
until we find this thing
sitting on our couch
curled up in a ball
under our favorite blanket
and munching on popcorn
as it watches television

we might ask
"how did you get in here?"

but it always answers with a smile
"I've been here all along."

(serendipity)

growth takes time
just ask the trees

growth takes patience
just ask the bees

growth comes in waves
just ask the sea

but in the end it's worth it
just ask me

if you ever wonder
what kinds of things
go through my head

read my poems

any poem

then you will know

1991

Angela is driving the Volkswagen
she's recently painted with flowers
along the coast of California
as "Down Under" plays on the radio
two hitchhikers are singing off-key
in the backseat
flowers in their hair
and stars in their eyes
as they munch on stale Doritos
and share a Styrofoam cup
of gas station coffee
they have no place to call home
a feeling she knows all too well
just two nomadic souls
wandering the continent
with a passion greater
than anything Angela has ever seen

she lets them stay with her
for exactly five days
before their wanderlust
gets the best of them again
and they part ways on the interstate

but those songs
those wilted flowers
and those Dorito crumbs on the floor
stay with her
to the end of her days

out with the old

in with the new

life can change

and so can you

I am the girl
who made a peace sign
in her mother's womb
I am the girl
with love in her name
and love in her heart
I am the girl
with stars and fire
shining in her eyes
I am the girl
who fights every day
just to stay alive
I am the girl
who bears her scars
inside and out
I am the girl
who doesn't speak
yet has so much to say
I am the girl
who chases sunsets
instead of boys
I am the girl
who no longer wants to
fit into a society gone mad

yes
I am just a girl
trying to be the change
I wish to see in the world

and learning how to love
who I have been
who I am
and who I will become

(wish me luck)

Acknowledgements:

First of all, I can't believe I'm even writing this right now. For years, releasing a book into the world was only a mere daydream that for the longest time I believed would never come true. But I was determined to tell my story, so I grabbed a pen and a pencil and etched my soul onto these pages until I gained the courage to just go for it.

Second of all, this isn't a typical acknowledgements page because this book was mostly kept secret, meaning that I did everything—inside and out—on my own. Of course, I did have some encouragement, and I couldn't be more grateful for my inspirations such as:

My other half, Tyler, who has always loved and supported me and helped me achieve my biggest dreams just by allowing me to be myself. And buying a laptop so I could write. And helping me with the whole formatting/editing process. And simply existing.

My bestie, Tanairi, who helped me get the ball rolling on my self-publishing journey and who has always been one of my biggest cheerleaders.

All of my wonderful family and friends (including the ones I have yet to meet) who have supported and continue to support me, and even the slithering snakes who don't (especially, actually.)

And, most of all, you. However you came across them, thank you for choosing my words. I promise there will be more to come.

Love,

Anna

Made in the USA
Columbia, SC
17 July 2025

60823259R00089